# "I Can Draw" CARTOON ANIMALS

Illustrated by Mary Grace Eubank

Hi! I'm Tippy the Pencil! I'm going to help you use this book. Whenever you see me, I'll give you hints on how to improve your drawing or have more fun.

Walter Foster

# Here's what you need...

You're about to become an artist! Before you start, make sure you have a pencil, a pencil sharpener, an eraser, a felt-tip pen, and one or more of the different coloring media pictured here.

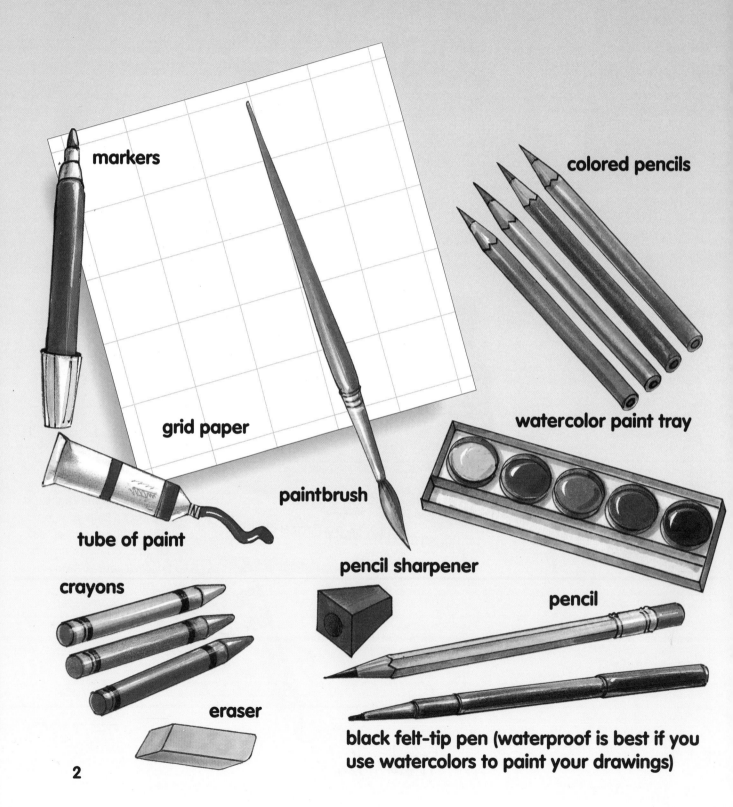

markers

colored pencils

grid paper

watercolor paint tray

paintbrush

tube of paint

pencil sharpener

crayons

pencil

eraser

black felt-tip pen (waterproof is best if you use watercolors to paint your drawings)

# And here's what you do!

**1** Copy each step-by-step drawing onto your grid paper, noticing where the drawing should touch the lines on your grid. Draw lightly in pencil. Since each new step is shown in blue, you'll always know exactly what to do next.

**2** You may erase the pencil construction lines as you go along so that you can see how your drawing is progressing. When you have finished, use your felt-tip pen to go over the lines you want to keep, and erase any stray pencil lines.

Now you have a perfect drawing to color any way you'd like! Before you color, you may want to read pages 30 - 32 for some extra coloring tips.

# Wiggles the Snake

Draw the snake's body and head with curved lines. Place his eyes at the top of his head.

**1**

Add a pattern to your snake's body, and give him pupils and eyelashes, a tongue and a lollipop.

**2**

Use your felt-tip pen to trace over the lines you want to keep, and erase the extra pencil lines.

**3**

**4** Color your snake!

4

# Jimmy Giraffe

Add details to the head and body and dress your giraffe in a turtleneck sweater.

Draw the head, neck, body, and legs. Add two small circles at the top of the head for eyes.

**1**

**2**

Use your felt-tip pen to trace over the lines you want to keep, and erase the extra pencil lines.

**3**

**4** Color your giraffe!

5

# Itty Bitty Kitty

Draw two overlapping circles for the body and head, and smaller curved shapes for front and back legs.

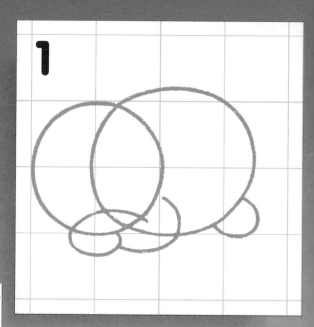

**1**

Draw another front leg, eyes, a nose, and a mouth.

**2**

Give your cat pointed ears and a curved tail and add more definition to the top of the head. Draw a small circle and oval to make the bird's head and body.

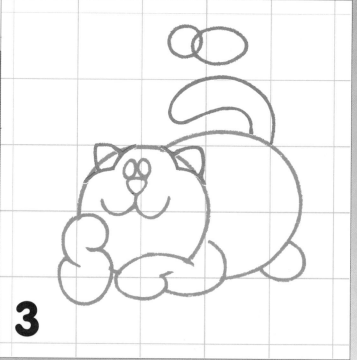

**3**

6

**4** Draw the toes and pupils and add details to the ears and face. Complete your cat with rough outlines to show fur. Finish the bird with a wing, eyes, a beak, legs, and a tail.

**5** Use your felt-tip pen to trace over the lines you want to keep, and erase the extra pencil lines.

**6** Color your cat!

# Ella Elephant

Draw a large circle for the elephant's body, and add the head, legs, and trunk.

**1**

**2**

Add the elephant's tutu, and give her arms, eyes, and a mouth.

Give your elephant ears, and shape the end of the trunk and the chin. Draw a wavy line to show the tutu's ruffle.

**3**

**4** Finish your drawing with details such as toes, a hairbow, pupils, and a tail. Balance your elephant on a ball.

Use your felt-tip pen to trace over the lines you want to keep, and erase the extra pencil lines.

**5**

It's a good idea to erase some of the construction lines as you go along.

**6** Color your elephant!

# Making Backgrounds

Drawing cartoon animals is even more fun when you add backgrounds. Your characters can appear in these settings, or you can switch the backgrounds for some funny results. How would the alligator look hanging from a banana tree?

Learn to draw the cat on page 6. ▶

Learn to draw the squirrel on page 28. ▲

**yarn**

**leaf**

Learn to draw the giraffe on page 5. ▲

Learn to draw the alligator on page 26. ▲

▼ Learn to draw the chimp on page 12:

twig

banana

11

# Impy Chimp

**1**

Draw the chimp's rounded body, head, and muzzle, and give him a long tail ending in a ball shape.

**2**

Add long curving limbs and add another loop to the chimp's tail. Use small semi-circles to draw his eyes and nose.

**3**

Draw floppy ears, the tip of the nose, and fingers. Add definition to the chimp's mouth, and add the narrow branch on either side of your chimp's tail.

Finish your chimp drawing with details on the face and limbs. Give him a banana in one hand and a cap in the other. Add leaves on the branch.

**4**

**5**

Use your felt-tip pen to trace over the lines you want to keep, and erase the extra pencil lines.

**6** Color your chimp!

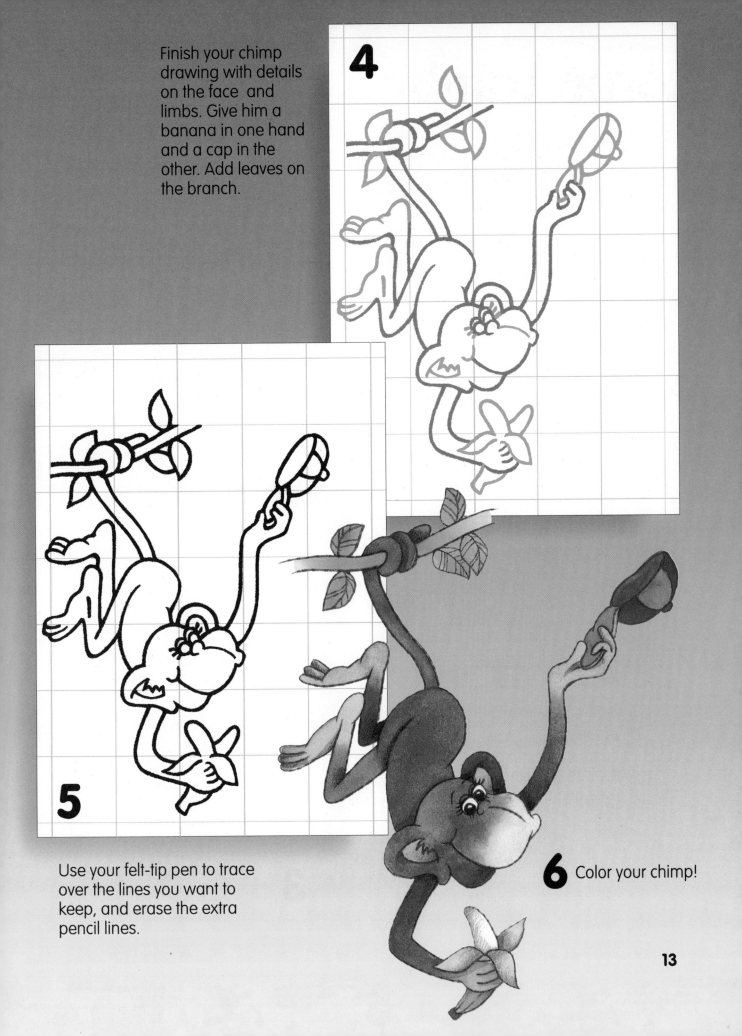

# Lorna Lamb

Draw the lamb's head, body, and legs.

**1**

Add the arms, skate blades, and cuff on the hat. Draw the eyes and mouth.

**2**

Give your lamb a scarf and tail, and form the top of the boots. Add details on the face and arms.

**3**

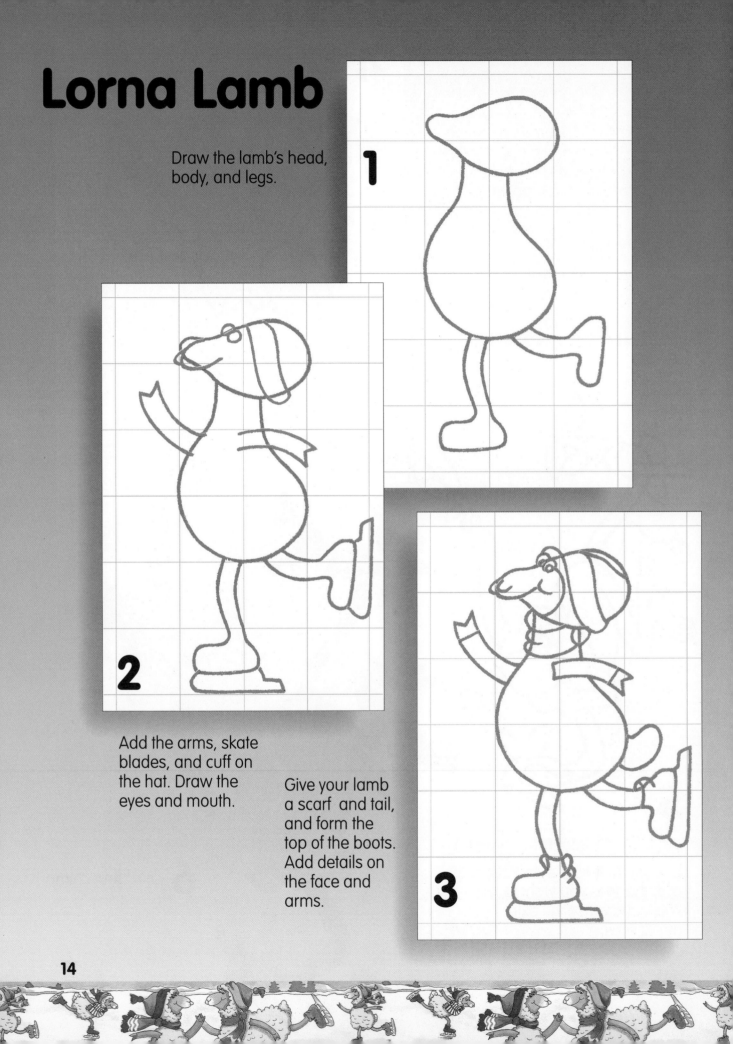

**4** Use lots of tiny curved lines to look like wool. Finish the ice skates, scarf, and hat.

**5** Use your felt-tip pen to trace over the lines you want to keep, and erase the extra pencil lines.

**6** Color your lamb!

# Runny Bunny

Draw an oversized oval for the head, and a smaller oval for the body. Add the legs.

Add the bunny's long ears, arms, neck, and feet. Shape the top of his head.

Use small circles to draw the eyes, nose, and tail. Give your bunny a T-shirt and big front teeth.

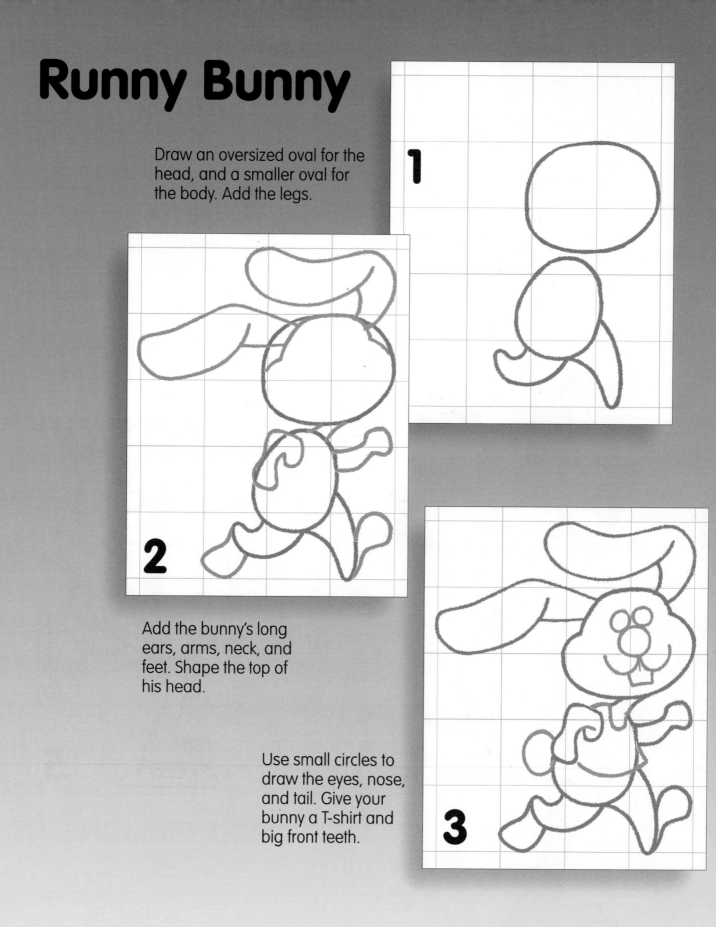

Finish your bunny with short, rough lines all around to indicate fur, and add details to the eyes, hands, and ears. Put a number "1" on his shirt.

Use your felt-tip pen to trace over the lines you want to keep, and erase any stray pencil lines.

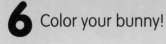

**6** Color your bunny!

# Cartoons in Action

You can use a variety of techniques to show your cartoon animals in action. Change the positions of their arms and legs, and indicate movement with short, brisk lines behind them. Another way to bring your drawing to life is to give your cartoon animals props, such as a hula hoop to spin or acorns to juggle.

# Bully Bulldog

**1** Draw rounded shapes for the bulldog's head and body. Add a front leg on the right side.

Add two more legs. Use curved lines to indicate your bulldog's jaws and forehead.

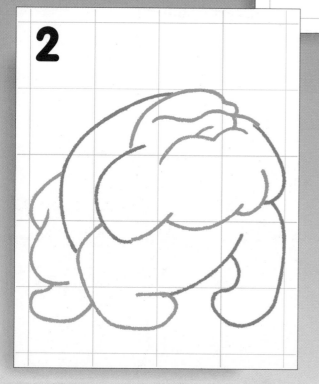

**2**

Give your bulldog eyes, teeth, and a thick lower lip. Give his legs more definition.

**3**

Finish your bulldog with more details such as spikes on his collar, toes, ears, a tail, and a bone in his mouth.

Use your felt-tip pen to trace over the lines you want to keep, and erase the extra pencil lines.

**4**

**5**

**6** Color your bulldog!

# Dinah Dino

Use long, curved lines to draw the dinosaur's body, head, and rear leg.

**1**

Give your dinosaur a tail, another leg, an arm, eyes, and a chin.

**2**

Add lines to define the dinosaur's tail, legs, and neck. Draw her mouth, another arm and the frame of the butterfly net. Add definition to the top of her head.

**3**

Complete your drawing by adding short, curved lines to the dinosaur's tail, neck , and legs. Give your dinosaur toes, and place a butterfly on her nose.

**4**

**5**

Use your felt-tip pen to trace over the lines you want to keep, and erase the extra pencil lines.

You can turn Dinah into a dragon by adding triangles down her back and a flame coming from her mouth.

**6** Color your dinosaur!

**tree**

**road**

**flowers**

# Putting It All Together

Once you've learned to draw different cartoon animals, you may want to put them in a picture together. You can create lots of interesting scenes to show off your artistic abilities. Try drawing your characters in different poses and sizes and in a variety of backgrounds. You can even make up stories to go with your pictures!

# Terminator Alligator

Start by using curved lines to draw the alligator's torso, head, and arms.

**1**

**2**

Add the alligator's legs, hands, and facial features.

Give your alligator a tail and muscles on his arms, and shape his long snout. Dress him in a T-shirt.

**3**

Finish your drawing by giving your alligator sharp teeth, lines across his stomach, spikes on his tail, and a barbell in his hands.

**4**

**5**

Use your felt-tip pen to trace over the lines you want to keep, and erase the extra pencil lines.

**6** Color your alligator!

# Acorn the Squirrel

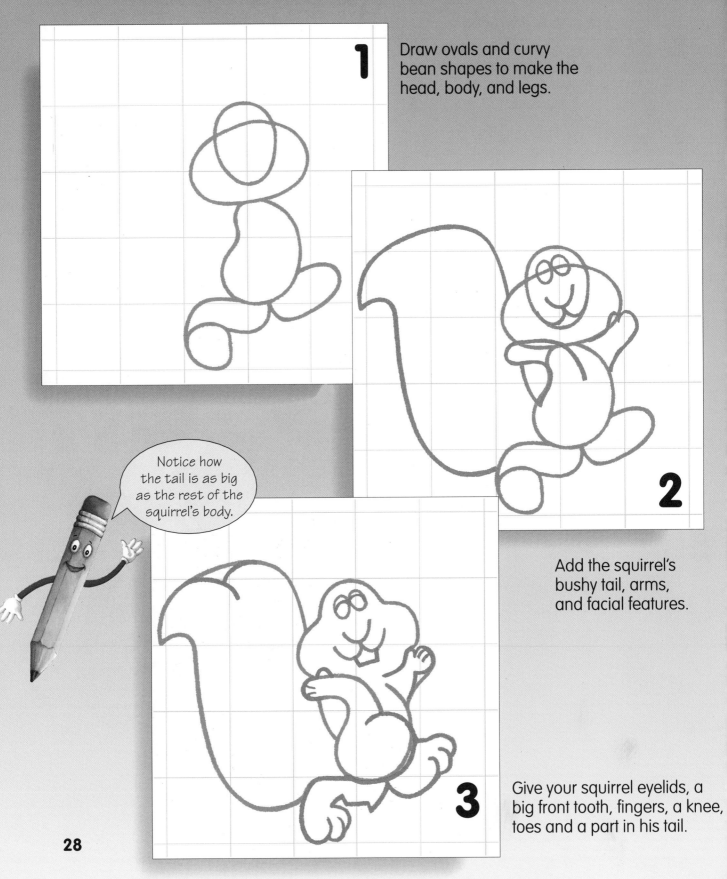

**1** Draw ovals and curvy bean shapes to make the head, body, and legs.

Notice how the tail is as big as the rest of the squirrel's body.

**2** Add the squirrel's bushy tail, arms, and facial features.

**3** Give your squirrel eyelids, a big front tooth, fingers, a knee, toes and a part in his tail.

**4** Add details by drawing circles for the squirrel's pupils, a long curved line for the underside of his tail, jagged lines for fur, and cheeks. Draw the acorns.

**5**

Use your felt-tip pen to trace over the lines you want to keep, and erase the extra pencil lines.

**6** Color your squirrel!

# Coloring Your Drawings

Once you've finished the outlines of your drawings, it's fun to color them in. Use watercolor paints, colored pencils, crayons, markers, or anything else you can think of!

Watercolors are fun to use, but sometimes when two wet paint colors are next to one another, they run together. If you're using watercolors, you might want to let the paint dry after each color you use.

Turn to the next page to learn a really special way to bring your drawings to life!

Markers give your drawings a smooth, bright finish and even colors.

Crayons and colored pencils are good for shading. See page 32 to learn how!

# Shading Your Drawings

Shading can add dimension and life to your drawings. When coloring your cartoon animals, leave some areas lighter than others to show where the light would shine. Then try shading with a crayon or colored pencil and watch your drawing come to life!

Use these grid pages for your drawings. Make extra copies so you can draw lots of pictures using the special steps in this book!